GW01393067

# Measures

## David Kirkby

### Heinemann

First published in Great Britain by Heinemann Library
an imprint of Heinemann Publishers (Oxford) Ltd
Halley Court, Jordan Hill, Oxford OX2 8EJ

MADRID ATHENS PARIS
FLORENCE PRAGUE WARSAW
PORTSMOUTH NH CHICAGO SAO PAULO
SINGAPORE TOKYO MELBOURNE AUCKLAND
IBADAN GABORONE JOHANNESBURG

Designed by The Point
Cover design by Pinpoint Design
**Printed in Hong Kong.**

00
10 9 8 7 6 5 4 3 2

ISBN 0431 06902 6

**British Library Cataloguing in Publication Data**
Kirkby, David
Measures and Space. - (Maths Live Series)
I. Title II. Series
510

Acknowledgements
The author and publisher wish to acknowledge, with thanks,
the following photographic sources:

Roger Scruton p5; Photoair p18; Colorsport p19; Allsport pp26, 27; Courtesy of Marconi p43;
Trevor Clifford pp8, 15, 17, 24, 35; L. Kamen p24.
Extract from Ordnance Survey on page 33 has been reproduced with the permission of the controller of
Her Majesty's Stationery Office © Crown Copyright: 1:50 000 Landranger showing Exeter and surround.

The publishers would also like to thank the following for the kind loan of equipment:
NES Arnold Ltd; Polydron International Ltd.

Note to reader: words in **bold** in the text are explained in the glossary on page 44.

# CONTENTS

# ANGLE

An **angle** is an amount of turn.

Claire turns through angles of one quarter turn, then another quarter turn, then another, and then one more until she is back facing the front again. Altogether she has turned through one whole turn. When we see her back, the angle she has turned through is one half turn.

The drawing shows the direction in which the hands of a clock turn. This direction is called a **clockwise** turn. A turn in the opposite direction is called an **anti-clockwise** turn.

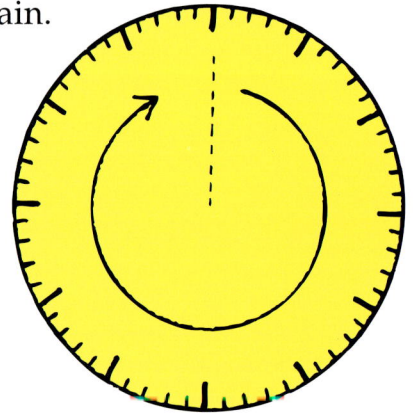

## TO DO:

**Play the turning game**

- Shuffle a pack of playing cards without the picture cards, and place them face down in a pile.
- Draw a large clock face.
- Start by placing a counter above '12'.
- Turn the top card over. Count a matching number of spaces round the clock, clockwise if the card is red, anti-clockwise if it is black, and place another counter where you land. Now turn over the next card, and repeat the process.
- Continue until all numbers except one have a counter beside them. For your score, count how many cards you needed.
- Play again, starting at a different number.

*The roundabout is turning in the direction that the horses are facing. Is it turning clockwise or anti-clockwise?*

The drawing shows the angle moved by the minute hand of a clock in 25 minutes. It is usual to draw a small arc to show the angle which has been turned.

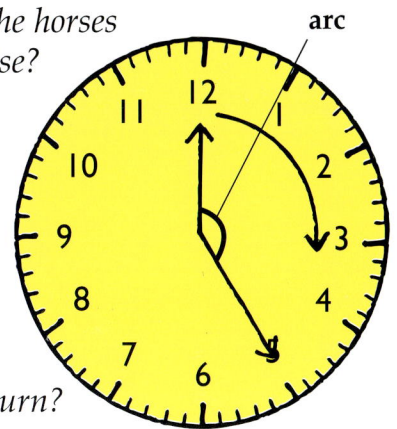

arc

*How many minutes pass when the hand turns through an angle of one quarter turn? One half turn?*

## TO DO:

### Make an angle demonstrator

You need a square piece of card and a paper fastener. You also need to make a pointer from card.

- Push the fastener through both the pointer and the card.
- Twist the pointer so that it turns easily. Use your demonstrator to show quarter turns, half turns, three-quarter turns and complete turns both clock-wise and anti-clockwise.

# 2 RIGHT ANGLES

An angle which is a quarter turn is called a **right angle**. We say that a quarter turn measures 1 right angle. A half turn measures 2 right angles. A three quarter turn measures 3 right angles. One complete turn measures 4 right angles.

The angles between the walls of a house are usually built so that all the corners are right angles.

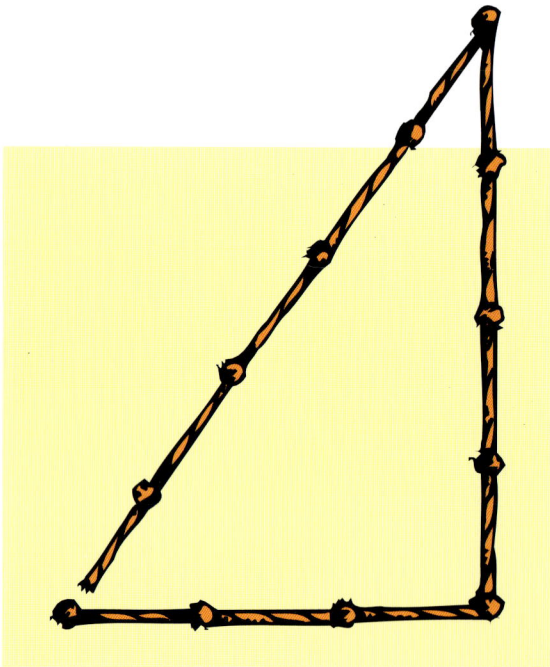

Ancient Egyptian builders used to make right angles by putting twelve equally spaced knots in a rope. They had discovered that they could use this to measure right angles. One builder held the two end knots together, another pulled the fourth knot from one end, while a third builder pulled the fifth knot from the other end. When they all pulled tightly, the rope made a right angle, which they could use to make sure their corners were right angles.

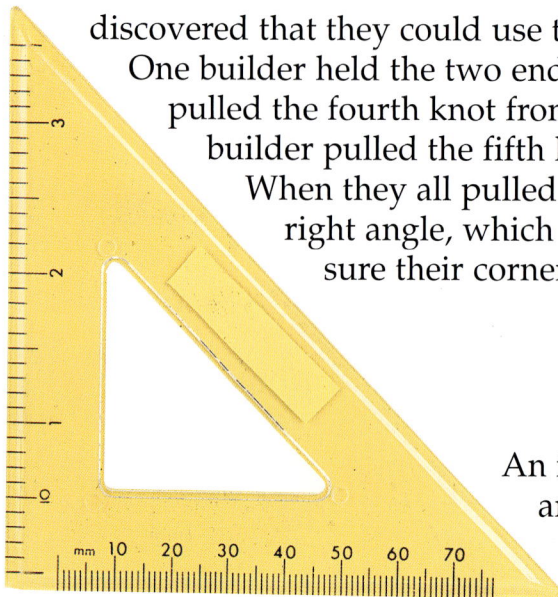

An instrument for drawing and checking right angles is called a **set-square**.

Some shapes have **vertices** which make right angles. It is usual to show these angles by drawing a small square.

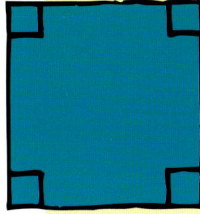

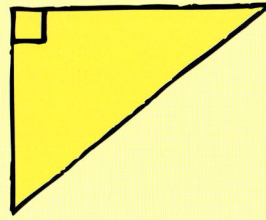

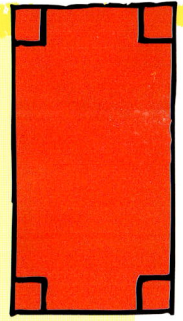

The angles of all four vertices of a square and a rectangle are right angles.

## CHALLENGE:

The first shape has 4 right angles, the second has 5 right angles. Can you draw a shape with 6 right angles?

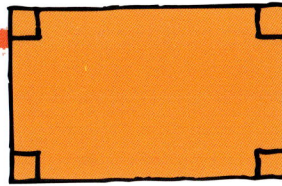

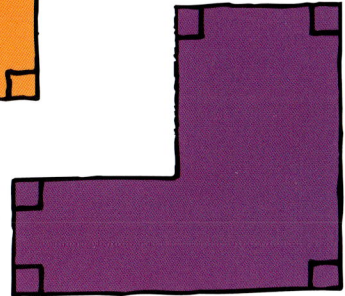

## CHALLENGE:

The clock shows 9 o'clock. The angle between the hands of the clock is 1 right angle. Can you list the times when the angle between the hands is 1 right angle? What about 2 right angles?

## TO DO:

### Make a right angle measure

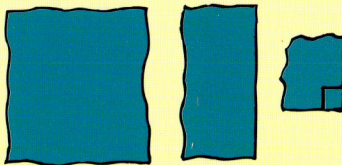

- Take a piece of scrap paper and fold it in half, and then in half again.
- You now have a right angle.
- Use it to test for right angles around you.

# TYPES OF ANGLE

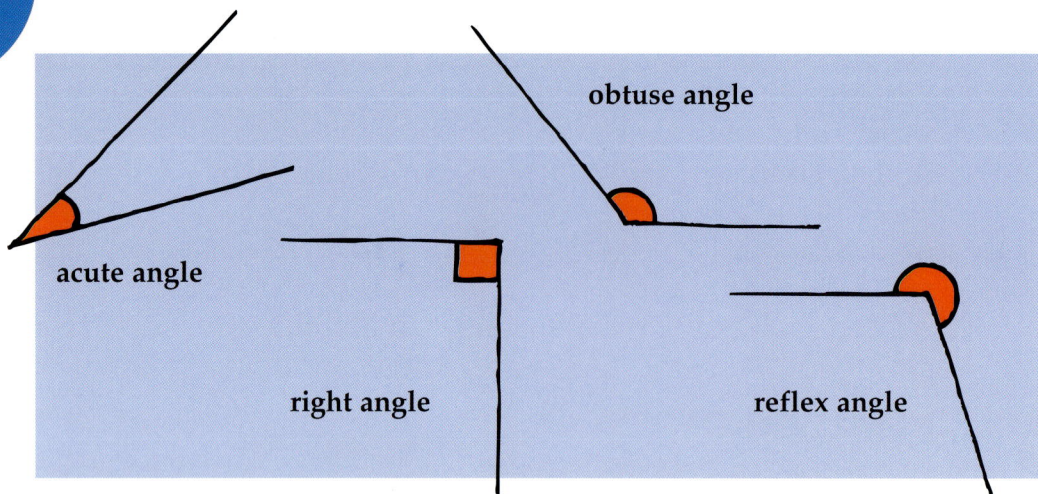

obtuse angle

acute angle

right angle

reflex angle

An angle which is less than 1 right angle is called an **acute angle**. An angle which is more than 1 right angle and less than 2 right angles is called an **obtuse angle**. An angle which is more than 2 right angles is called a **reflex angle**.

*What type of angles are there between the spokes of the umbrella?*

Siobhan has made a right angle with her book open, and Paul has made an obtuse angle.

## CHALLENGE:

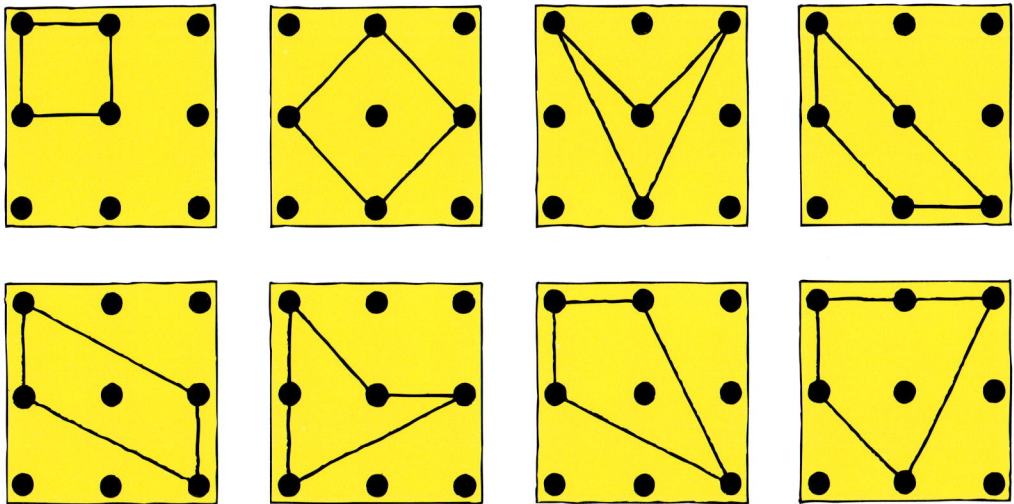

Can you say what types of angle each shape has?

## CHALLENGE:

It is 1 o'clock. The smallest angle between the hands of the clock is an acute angle. There are two 'o'clock' times when the angle between the hands is a right angle, four when it is an acute angle, and four when it is an obtuse angle. What are they?

## TO DO:

**Make an angle turner**

You need two different-coloured circles of paper.
- Cut a straight line from the edge to the centre of each circle.
- Slot the two circles together through the cut lines, so that the circles are on top of each other.
- Turn one of the circles to show different-sized angles.
- Show acute angles, obtuse angles and reflex angles.

# 4 MEASURING ANGLE

We measure angles in **degrees**.

There are 90 degrees in one right angle.
Mathematical shorthand for writing 90 degrees is 90°.

So a quarter turn is 1 right angle = 90°
a half turn is 2 right angles = 180°
a three quarter turn is 3 right angles = 270°
a whole turn is 4 right angles = 360°

The ancient Egyptians believed that the Sun moved round the Earth, taking one year of 360 days to complete the journey. This was the reason for dividing one complete turn into 360 degrees.

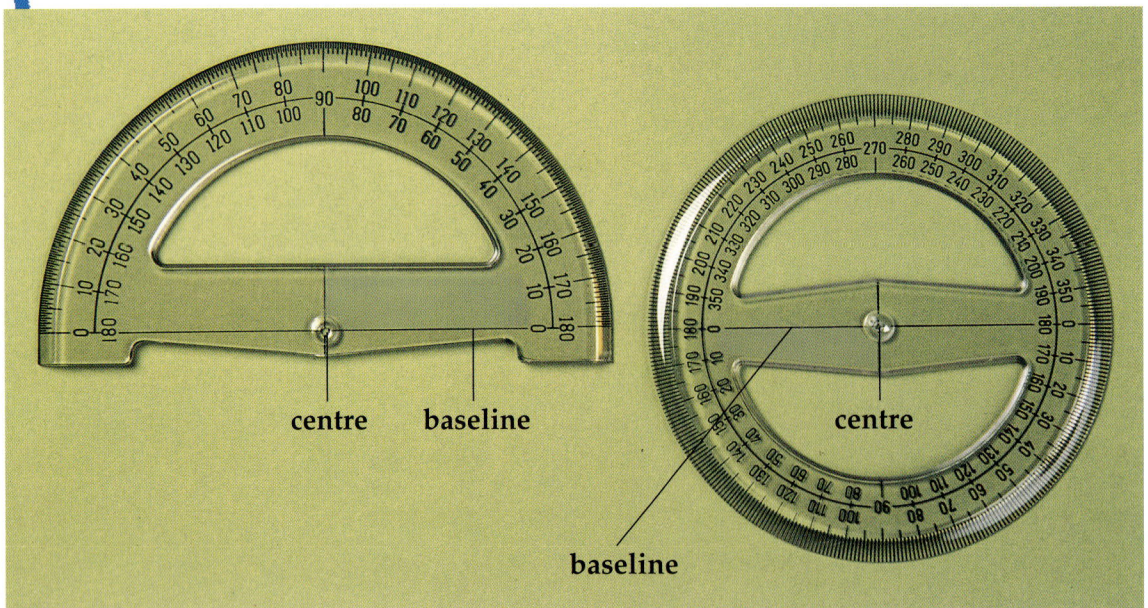

centre    baseline                              centre

baseline

An instrument for measuring angle is called a **protractor**. A **semi-circular protractor** is called a 180° protractor because it spans 2 right angles. A **circular protractor** is called a 360° protractor because it spans 4 right angles.

The protractor has two scales – an inside scale and an outside scale – which are graded in opposite directions. On the 180° protractor, each scale starts at 0° and ends at 180°. Each protractor has a **baseline** and a **centre**.

## TO DO:

**Measure an angle**

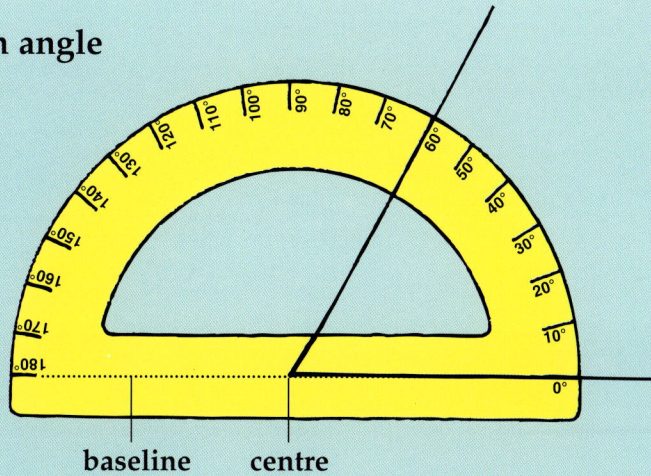

baseline    centre

- Place the centre of the protractor on the meeting point of the two arms of the angle, and the baseline along one arm.
- Look at the scale which starts at 0° at the end of the arm, then read round the scale to find the angle.
- What is the angle measured?

It is a good idea to estimate the size of the angle before you measure it.

## TO DO:

**Play the angle estimation game**

You need a partner.

- Draw two straight lines, meeting at an angle, using a ruler.
- Estimate the size of the angle in degrees.
- Use a protractor to measure its size accurately.
- The winner is the player whose estimate is closest.

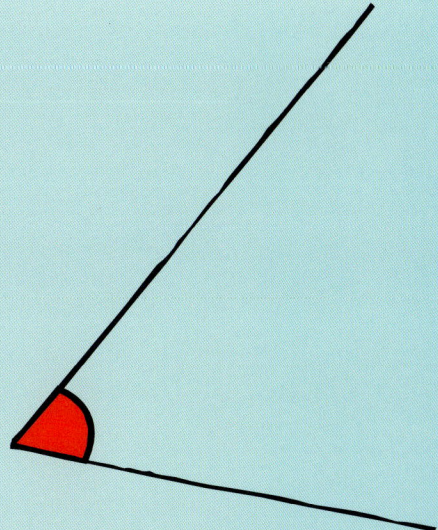

# 5 ANGLES OF POLYGONS

Here are some different **polygons**.
The angles in each polygon have been marked.

triangle          quadrilateral          pentagon   hexagon

The triangle has 3 angles, the quadrilateral has 4, the pentagon has 5 and the hexagon has 6. The number of angles in a polygon matches the number of sides of a polygon.

When the 3 angles of a triangle are measured and then added together, the total is always 2 right angles or 180°.

## TO DO:

**Put the angles of a triangle together**

- Draw and cut out a large triangle from paper or card. Colour the three angles.
- Tear off the three corners which represent the three angles.
- Place them together with points touching.
- What is the total of the three angles?
- Try this again with a different type of triangle.

**Put the angles of a quadrilateral together**

- Draw and cut out a quadrilateral. Colour the four angles.
- Tear off the four angles, and place them together with points touching.
- What is the total of the four angles?

Another way to find the total of the angles of a shape is to divide it into triangles. A quadrilateral can be split into two triangles. The total of the angles of the quadrilateral is the same as the total of the angles of both triangles, which is two lots of 2 right angles, or 4 right angles altogether. This shows that the four angles of a quadrilateral total 4 right angles.

## CHALLENGE:

- Draw a pentagon (a 5-sided shape) and a hexagon (a 6-sided shape).
- Use the method of dividing a shape into triangles to show that the total of the angles in a pentagon is 6 right angles, and in a hexagon it is 8 right angles.

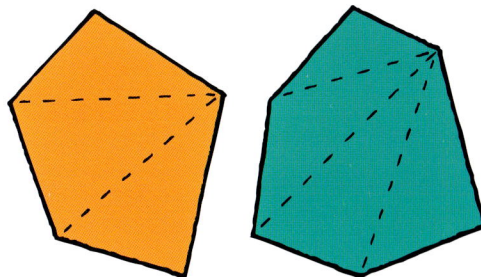

# 6 AREA

**Area** is a measure of the amount of surface space a **two-dimensional** object uses. *Which of these leaves do you think uses the most space on the page?*

The leaf which takes up the most space has the largest area. The leaf which takes up the least space has the smallest area.

Area is measured using squares because they fit neatly together, without leaving gaps (they **tessellate**). If squares of the same size are used to measure areas, it is easy to compare the areas of different shapes. A common size of square is one whose sides are 1 centimetre long. This unit of area is called a **square centimetre**.

To measure the area of the leaf, you count the number of whole squares inside the leaf. Can you find 11? This is close to the area of the leaf. We can be more accurate by including the squares which are partly inside the leaf. The rule is to count those squares which are more than half inside the leaf, and to ignore the others. Check that there are 7 squares which are more than half inside the leaf. So altogether the area of the leaf is 18 square centimetres.

Find the area of the island. The grid is marked in square kilometres.

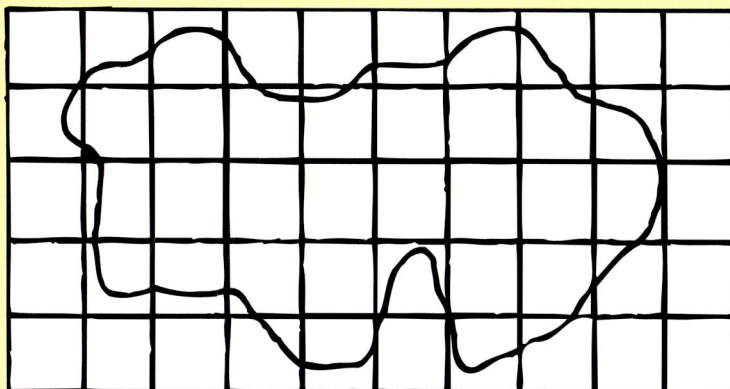

In mathematical shorthand, we write:

$cm^2$ for square centimetre.
$m^2$ for square metre.
$km^2$ for square kilometre.

Bejal is measuring the area of her hand. On centimetre squared paper, she has drawn round the outline of her hand. Then she can measure its area by counting the squares.

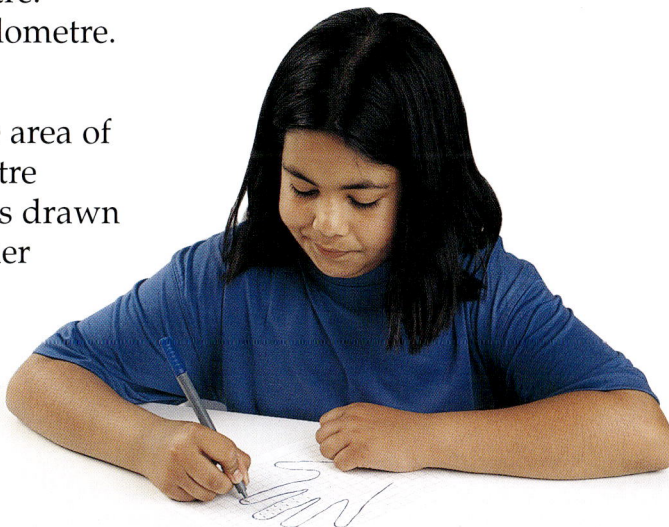

**TO DO:**

• Measure the area of one of your own hands, then the area of a friend's hand. Compare them.
• Find the area of the sole of your foot.

# 7 AREA OF A RECTANGLE

The area of a rectangle is measured by counting the number of squares inside the rectangle. *Which of these rectangles uses the most space on the paper?*

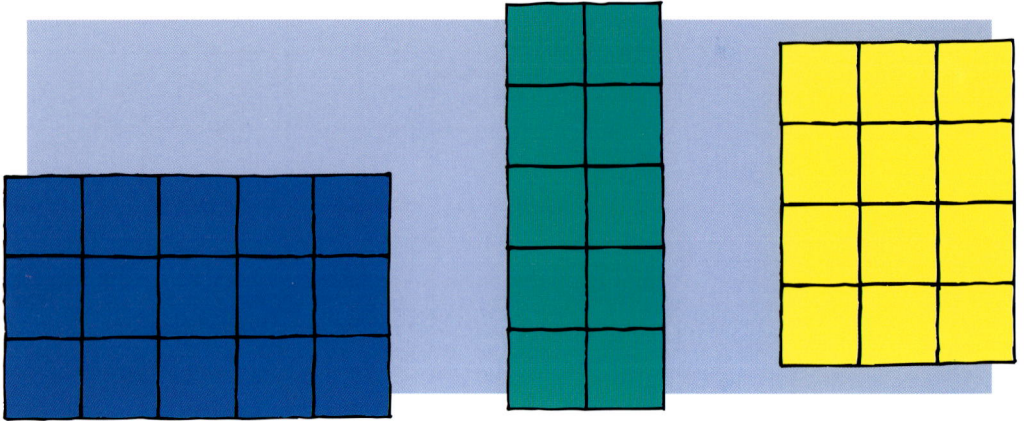

The blue rectangle has 3 rows of 5 squares, so its area is
$3 \times 5 = 15$ square centimetres (or 15 cm$^2$).
The green rectangle has 5 rows of 2 squares, so its area is
$5 \times 2 = 10$ square centimetres (or 10 cm$^2$).
The yellow rectangle has 4 rows of 3 squares, so its area is
$4 \times 3 = 12$ square centimetres (or 12 cm$^2$).

It is possible to find the areas of rectangles when the squares inside are hidden. Look at the red rectangle and imagine the square centimetres are drawn inside it. There will be 3 rows of 7 squares, so its area is $3 \times 7 = 21$ square centimetres (or 21 cm$^2$).
*What are the areas of the pink and grey rectangles?*

The areas of floors and walls in a house are measured in square metres. To measure the area of a rectangular-shaped floor, measure the length and width of the floor, in metres, then write it down.

So the area of the floor is 4 x 6 = 24 square metres (or 24 m²).

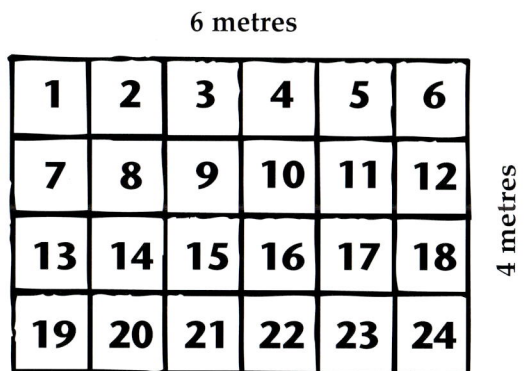

**6 metres**

| 1 | 2 | 3 | 4 | 5 | 6 |
|---|---|---|---|---|---|
| 7 | 8 | 9 | 10 | 11 | 12 |
| 13 | 14 | 15 | 16 | 17 | 18 |
| 19 | 20 | 21 | 22 | 23 | 24 |

**4 metres**

## TO DO:

On squared paper, draw five rectangles or squares with areas of 8, 9, 10, 11 and 12 square centimetres.

## CHALLENGE:

Can you draw three different rectangles, each with an area of 12 square centimetres?

# 8 PERIMETER

The **perimeter** of a shape is the distance around the boundary of the shape.

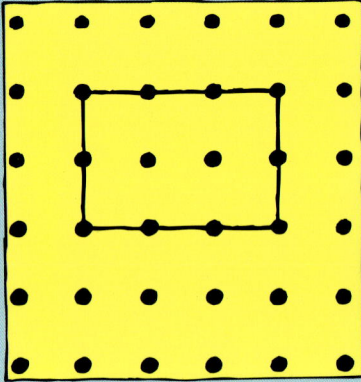

Perimeter is 10 units     Perimeter is 16 units     Perimeter is 14 units

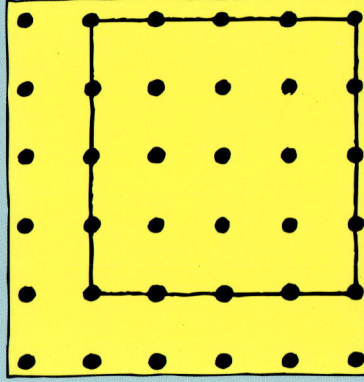

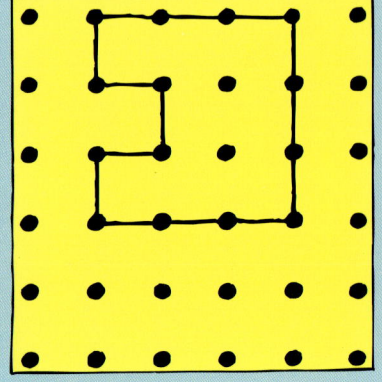

Check the perimeters of these shapes.

A farmer wants to put a fence all the way round his field. He needs to know the perimeter of his field, so that he knows how much fencing to buy.

A running track is marked out with straight and curved lines. Each lane lies between two of these lines. The lane nearest the centre of the track is called the inside lane. The lane furthest from the centre is called the outside lane. The perimeter of the inner line of the inside lane is 400 metres. So the perimeters for the other lanes are clearly more than 400 metres.

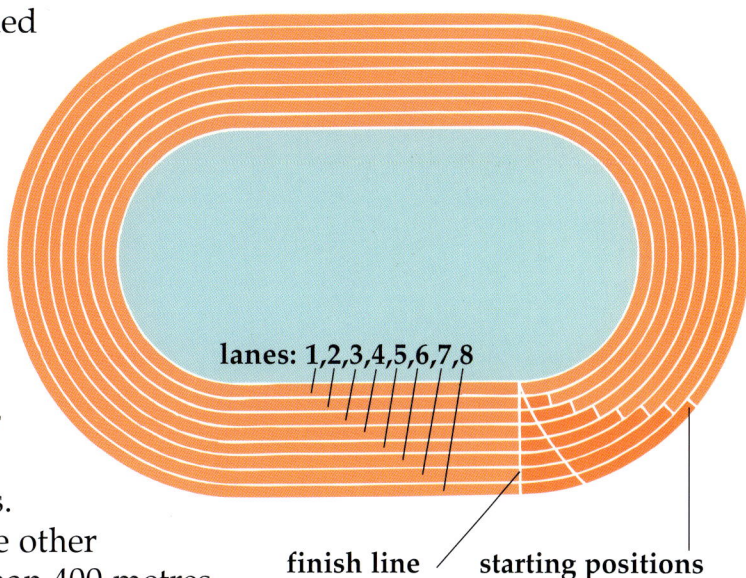

lanes: 1,2,3,4,5,6,7,8

finish line    starting positions

In a 400 metre race, each runner runs in their own lane. To make sure that each runner has exactly 400 metres to run, the runners start in different positions. The runners in the outer lanes start further forward. The starting positions are staggered.

## CHALLENGE:

You need a set of five equal-sized squares.

- Make shapes by joining some of the squares, edge to edge.
- Check that this shape has a perimeter of 10 units.
- Can you make five more different shapes, each with a perimeter of 10 units?
- You may use as many squares as you like to make your shapes.

# 9 VOLUME

**Volume** is a measure of the amount of space a solid **(three-dimensional)** object uses.

Each of these objects uses different amounts of space, so they have different volumes.

Volume and area both measure amounts of space. Area measures the amount of space used by a flat (two-dimensional) object. Volume measures the amount of space used by a solid (three-dimensional) object.

We use squares to measure area, and we use cubes to measure volume. This is because cubes fill three-dimensional space neatly, without leaving gaps (they tessellate).

There are 3 layers of 2 rows of 2 cubes in this box. The volume of the box is 12 stock cubes.

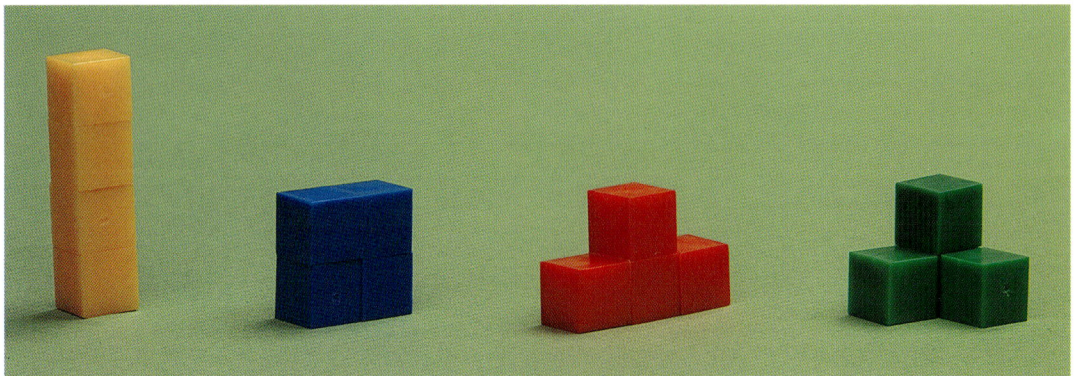

Here are some different buildings made from the same number of cubes. The volume of each building is 4 cubes.

When measuring volume, a **cubic centimetre** is sometimes used. This is a cube with edges which are 1 centimetre long.

The blue building has 3 layers of 2 rows of 5 cubic centimetres, so its volume is 3 x 2 x 5 = 30 cubic centimetres. *What is the volume of the other two buildings?*

When measuring area, we used mathematical shorthand to write $cm^2$ for square centimetre. When measuring volume, we use $cm^3$ for cubic centimetre. So the volume of the blue building is $30\,cm^3$. Sometimes we measure volume with larger cubes such as cubic metres, and we write $m^3$ in shorthand.

## CHALLENGE:

Can you find the volumes of these cuboids? Which has the smallest volume?

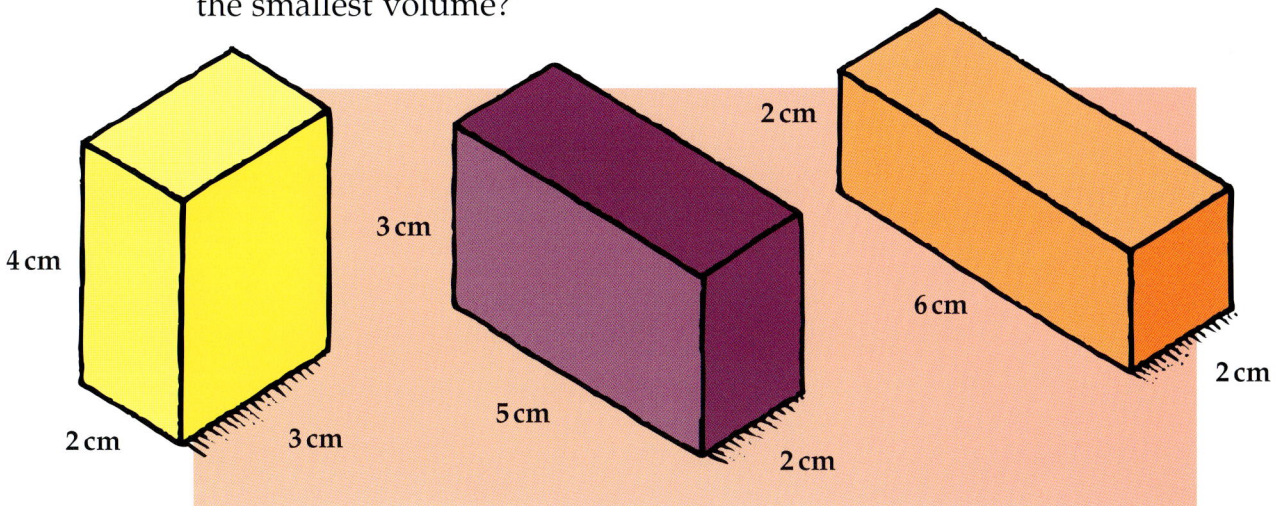

4 cm

3 cm

2 cm

2 cm

3 cm

5 cm

2 cm

2 cm

6 cm

2 cm

# 10 CAPACITY

**Capacity** is a measure of the volume of a container.

The amount of lemonade in a full bottle is called the capacity of the bottle. The amount of water in a full kettle is called the capacity of the kettle.

These cubes are built from squares of length 10 centimetres. The cube on the left can be built from 10 layers of 10 rows of 10 centimetre cubes. It has a volume of:
$10 \times 10 \times 10 = 1000$ cubic centimetres ($1000 \, cm^3$).

The open cube on the right has a capacity of 1000 cubic centimetres ($1000 \, cm^3$) of liquid. A capacity of 1000 cubic centimetres is also called a **litre** (written $1 \, l$).
The capacity of each small cubic centimetre is called a **millilitre** (written $1 \, ml$). The capacity of a row of 10 small cubic centimetres is called a **centilitre** (written $1 \, cl$).
So $1000 \, ml = 1 \, l$
$100 \, cl = 1 \, l$

When cooking from a recipe, we use a measuring jug to make sure we have the correct amount of water. These jugs are marked in millilitres.

The petrol pumped into a car petrol tank is measured in litres. The capacity of a petrol tank depends on the type of car. The cost of the petrol is a certain amount per litre.

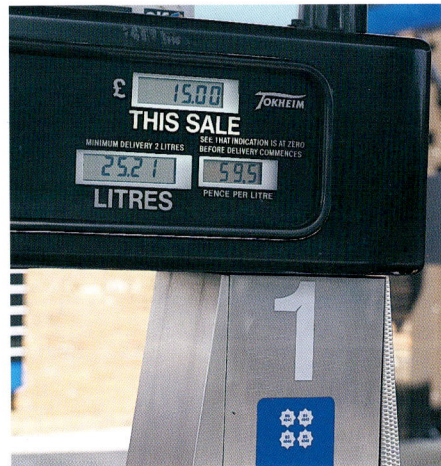

## TO DO:

- Find some containers in your kitchen which show their capacity.
- Make a list of the containers and their capacities.

| | |
|---|---|
| milk carton | 568ml |
| Squash bottle | 1l |
| kettle | 1.7l |
| washing-up liquid bottle | 600ml |

## CHALLENGE:

Can you work out how much liquid you drink each day?

# 11 HORIZONTAL AND VERTICAL

When you look at the picture above, you can see a line where the sky and sea seem to meet. This is called the horizon. A straight line drawn across a page from left to right is called a **horizontal** line. The word 'horizontal' comes from the word 'horizon'.

When you are standing upright, you are standing vertically. A **vertical** line is drawn straight up the paper.

Squared paper is made from a set of horizontal and vertical lines.

To check that a surface is horizontal, we use a spirit level. If the bubble can be seen in the centre of the glass window of the spirit level, then the table top is horizontal.

A plumb line is used to check that objects are vertical. It is a weight tied to the end of a piece of string, which, when still, will hang in a vertical direction. Builders need to make sure that the walls of buildings are vertical.

## TO DO:

- Write the capital letters from A to Z.
- Which letters have horizontal lines?
- Which have vertical lines?
- Which have both?

# 12 PARALLEL AND PERPENDICULAR

A set of **parallel lines** do not cross.
If the lines are continued at each end as far as you like, they will still not cross.

To show that lines are parallel, we draw an arrow on each parallel line.

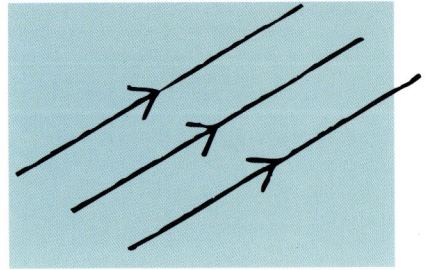

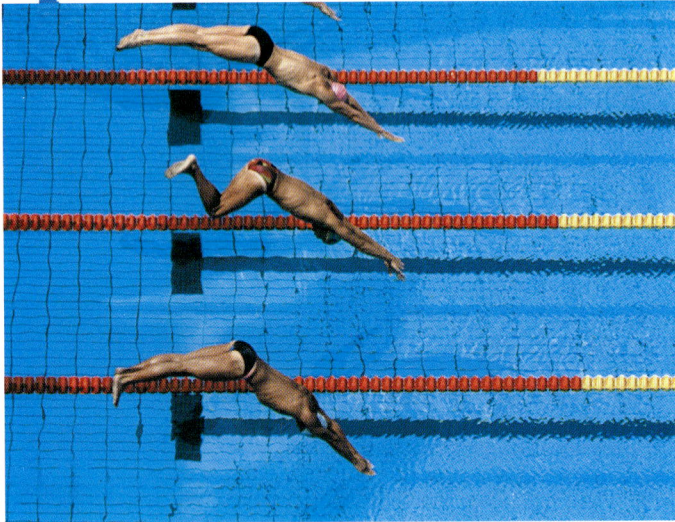

The lanes in a swimming pool are marked by parallel lines, and each lane is the same width.

Music is written on parallel lines.

There are many other parallel lines to be seen when you are outside. Examples are railway lines, double yellow line markings on the road, and telegraph lines.

**Perpendicular lines** are at right angles to each other.

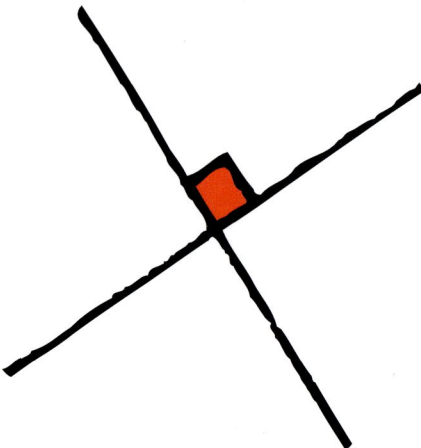

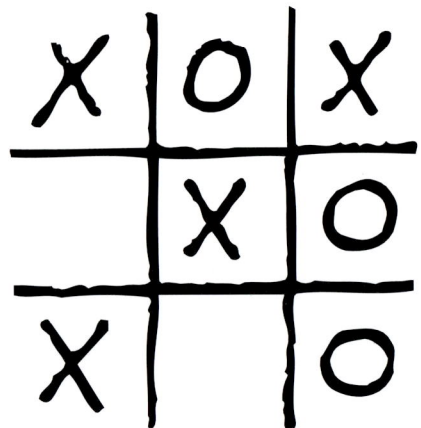

Horizontal and vertical lines are perpendicular to each other.

The horizontal bars are parallel to each other. They are perpendicular to the vertical stands which support them.

## TO DO:

**Use a set-square to draw a series of parallel lines**

- Draw a straight line.
- Then slide the set-square along the line, stopping it at different places to draw lines perpendicular to the original straight line.

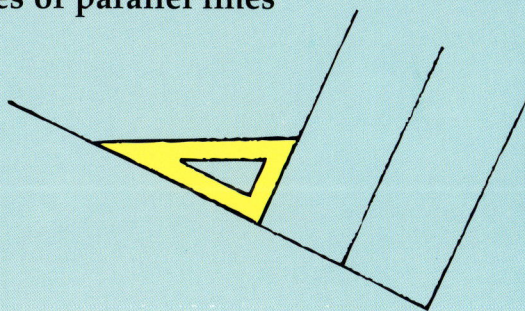

## CHALLENGE:

- Which of these shapes have parallel lines?
- Which have lines perpendicular to each other?

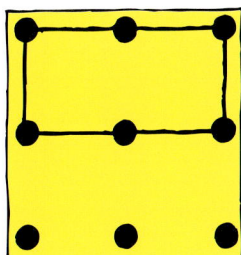

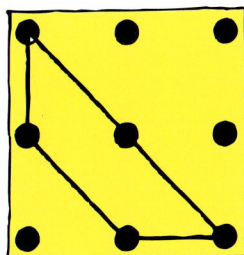

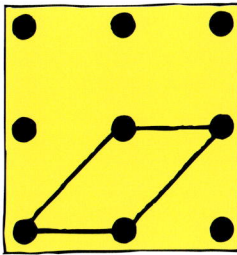

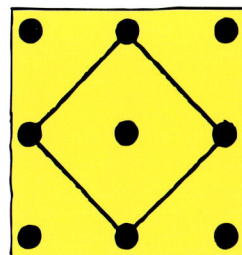

# 13 DIAGONAL LINES

A **diagonal** line is a straight line which joins two vertices of a shape.

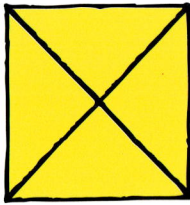

square

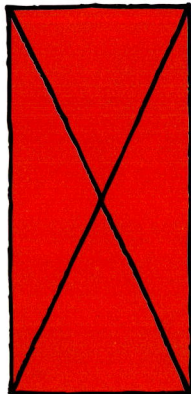

rectangle

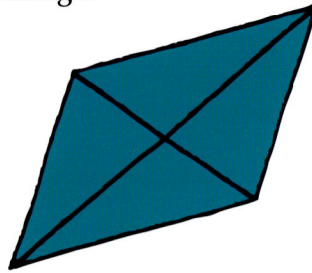

parallelogram

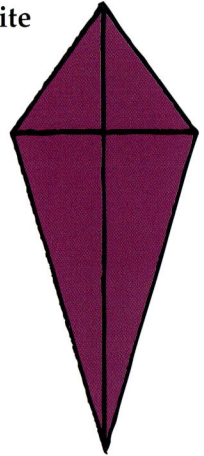

kite

All quadrilaterals can have two diagonals. The two diagonals of the square are the same length. They meet at right angles to each other. They are perpendicular. The two diagonals of the rectangle are also the same length, but they are not perpendicular. The diagonals of the parallelogram are of different lengths. The diagonals of a kite are of different lengths, but they are always perpendicular.

*Do you notice the pattern along this diagonal lines of numbers?*
*Can you spot patterns along another diagonal line of numbers?*

| 0 | 1 | 2 | 3 | 4 | 5 | 6 | 7 | 8 | 9 |
|---|---|---|---|---|---|---|---|---|---|
| 10 | 11 | 12 | 13 | 14 | 15 | 16 | 17 | 18 | 19 |
| 20 | 21 | 22 | 23 | 24 | 25 | 26 | 27 | 28 | 29 |
| 30 | 31 | 32 | 33 | 34 | 35 | 36 | 37 | 38 | 39 |
| 40 | 41 | 42 | 43 | 44 | 45 | 46 | 47 | 48 | 49 |
| 50 | 51 | 52 | 53 | 54 | 55 | 56 | 57 | 58 | 59 |
| 60 | 61 | 62 | 63 | 64 | 65 | 66 | 67 | 68 | 69 |
| 70 | 71 | 72 | 73 | 74 | 75 | 76 | 77 | 78 | 79 |
| 80 | 81 | 82 | 83 | 84 | 85 | 86 | 87 | 88 | 89 |
| 90 | 91 | 92 | 93 | 94 | 95 | 96 | 97 | 98 | 99 |

**TO DO:**

- Draw a regular pentagon, then draw all of its diagonals. How many are there?
- What about a regular hexagon?

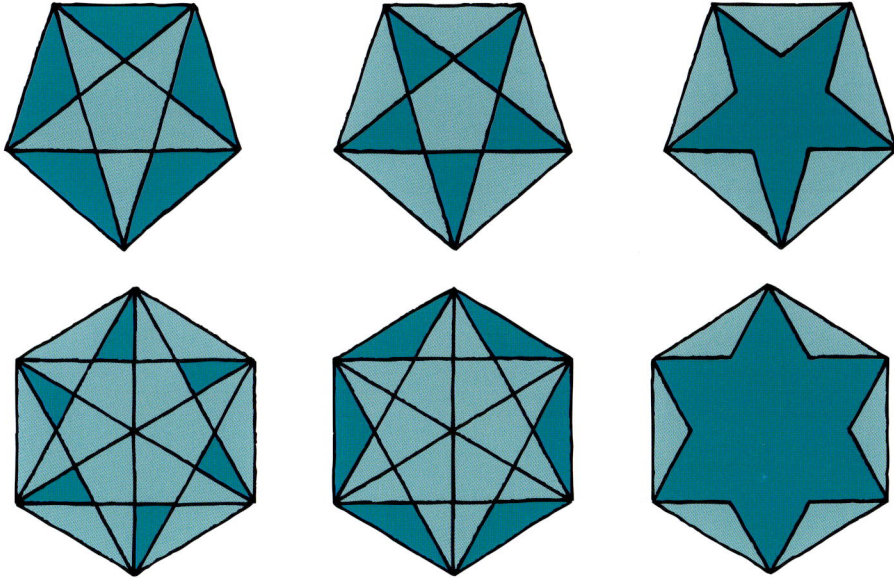

When the diagonals of a pentagon and hexagon are drawn, they can be used to make some interesting patterns.

**TO DO:**

- Draw and cut out a square.
- Draw both diagonals, then cut along these to make four triangles.
- Investigate the shape and size of these triangles. Are they the same or different?
- Now repeat the activity with some different 4-sided shapes, including a rectangle, a parallelogram and a kite.

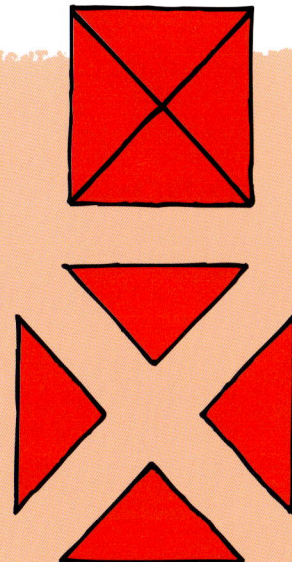

# 14 ENLARGING

Drawings or objects can be the same shape, but of different sizes. If we copy a shape but make the copy larger, it is called an **enlargement**.

Look at these two faces. The face on the right is an enlargement of the face on the left.

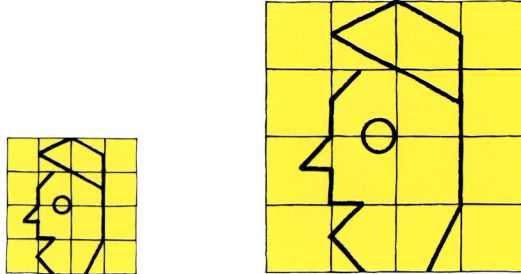

The lengths of the squares on the right are twice the lengths of the squares on the left. To make the enlargement, the drawing in each square on the left is copied on to each square on the right.
For example:

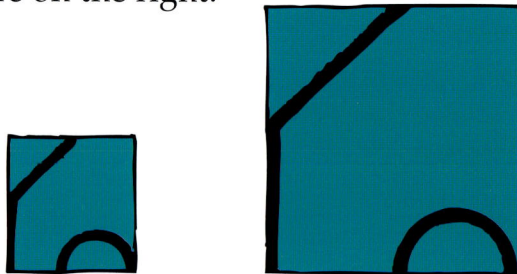

The lengths in the enlargement are twice the lengths in the smaller shape. It is a 'double-size enlargement' or a 'times 2 enlargement'.

## TO DO:

You need some squared paper.

- Copy this train on to the small squares.
- Outline some squares which are twice the length of the small squares.
- Draw a double-size enlargement of the train.

This set of Russian dolls is an example of enlarged three-dimensional (solid) shapes.

The middle cube is a double-size enlargement of the small cube. The cube on the right is a treble-size enlargement of the small cube.

## CHALLENGE:

- Can you work out how many small cubes are needed to build each cube in the picture?
- What about the next cube: a times 4 enlargement?

# 15 SCALE

A **plan** is a drawing of an object from above. Here is a plan of a kitchen. It is useful to draw a plan to help decide the best place to put the cooker, the washing machine, the fridge and other items.

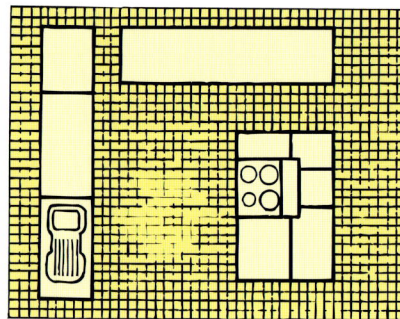

Scale drawings are used to show plans for buildings. This is a scale drawing of the plan of a bungalow.

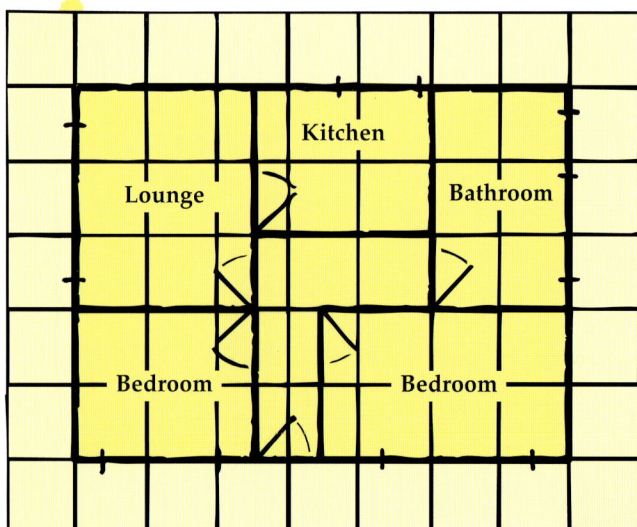

A distance of 1 centimetre on the drawing matches a distance of 1 metre on the bungalow. This means that 1 centimetre on the drawing matches 100 centimetres on the bungalow. We say the scale is 1 to 100. We often write this scale as 1:100. The drawing measurements are one hundredth of the bungalow measurements.

The football pitch is drawn to a scale of 1 in 1000 or 1:1000. This means that 1 centimetre on the drawing matches 10 metres on the pitch.

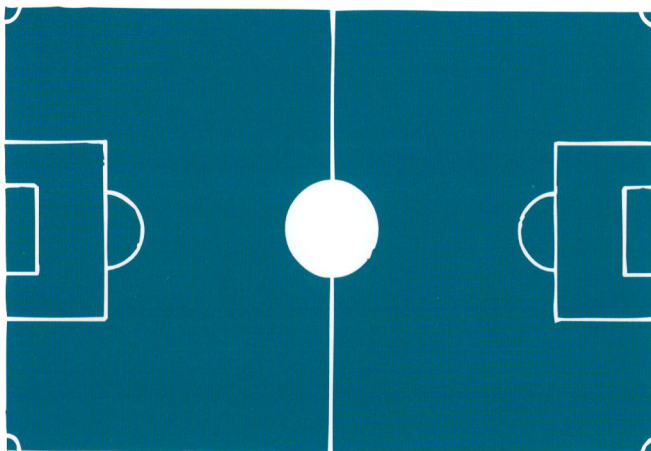

## TO DO:

Make a scale drawing of your bedroom. Use a scale of 1 to 50.

This map is drawn to scale. The scale is 1:50 000 or 1 in 50 000. This means that 1 centimetre on the map matches 50 000 centimetres on the land, which means that 1 centimetre matches 500 metres on the land. So 2 centimetres matches 1 kilometre.

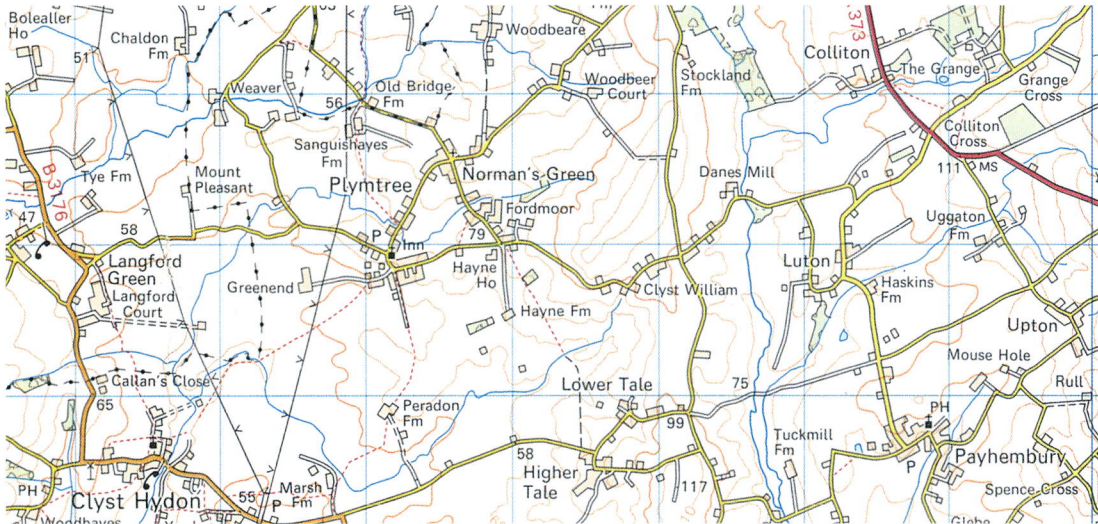

You can use a map drawn to scale, to work out distances between landmarks. To find out the distance between Norman's Green and Greenend, first use a ruler to measure the distance between them on the map, in centimetres. Check that it is about 3 centimetres.
Now this distance needs to be multiplied by 500 to give the real distance in metres.
So 3 x 500 = 1500 metres or 1.5 kilometres.

## TO DO:

- Use the map to find the distances, in metres, between:
  Mouse Hole and Danes Mill
  Mount Pleasant and Norman's Green.

- Find the distance, in metres, between your own choice of landmarks.

## CHALLENGE:

Can you find two places which are about 1000 metres apart?

# 16 VIEWS

Sometimes objects can look strange when viewed from different positions.

Here are some objects viewed from above.
*Do you know what each object is?*

*Do you recognize these objects?* This is probably easier because we are more used to viewing objects from the side than from above.

In the picture above, each person sees a different view of the cubes. The four different views are shown below. Can you work out who sees each view? Can you draw the view from above?

**TO DO:**

You need some cubes.

- Make a building by joining some cubes together.
- Draw four different views from the side, and draw the view from above.

# 17 GRIDS

A **grid** is a rectangle arrangement of squares.
It has a number of rows (across the grid) and a number of
columns (down the grid).

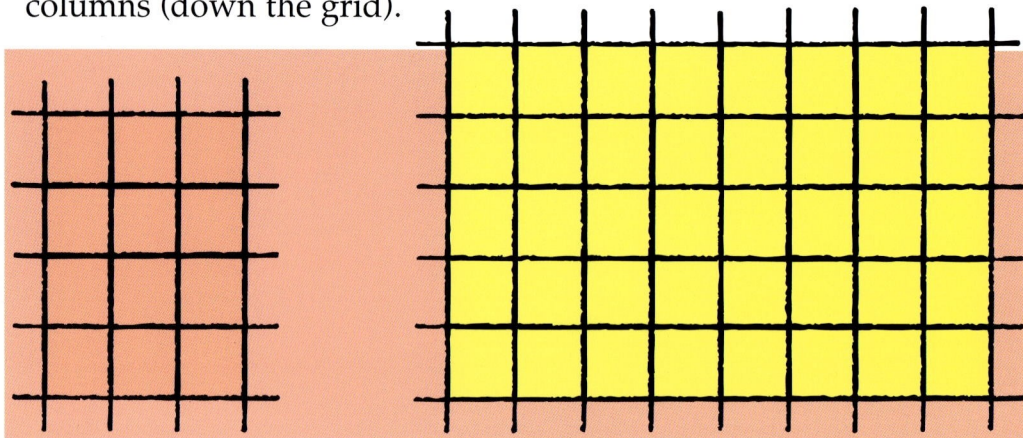

The pink grid has 4 rows and 3 columns, the yellow grid
has 5 rows and 8 columns.

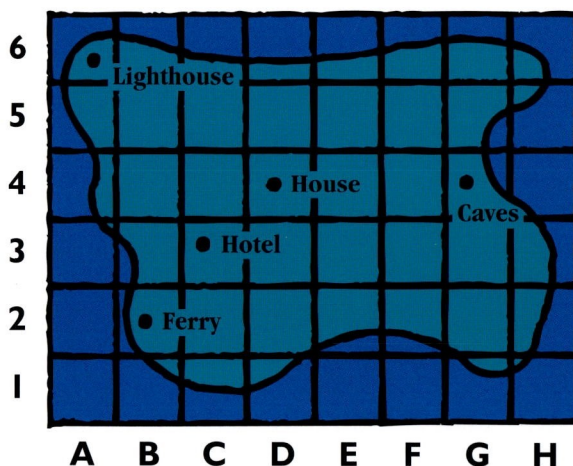

A map is usually marked with a grid so that the position
of places on the map can be found. Each row of the grid
above is labelled 1 to 6, and each column is labelled A to
H. Now each square on the grid can be labelled. The
house is positioned at D4. To find the house, look in
column D and also along row 4.

## CHALLENGE:

What is the position of the caves, lighthouse and the
hotel on the map, using letters and numbers?

# CHALLENGE:

To find the position of a road or street in a town, you can refer to the street map. Start by looking at the key to find the position of the road. For example, to find Hoober Road, the reference is A4 109. This shows that it can be found on page 109, and the grid reference is A4.

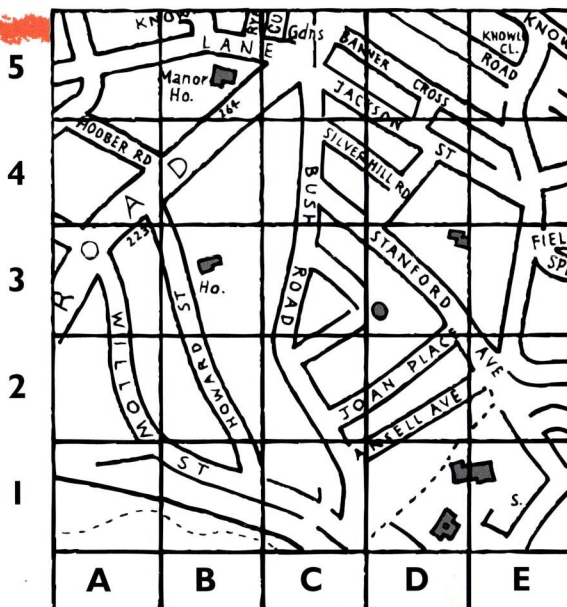

Can you find these streets on the map?

| | | | |
|---|---|---|---|
| Willow St | A2 109 | Howard St | B2 109 |
| Bush Rd | C4 109 | Silver Hill Rd | C4 109 |
| Ansell Ave | D2 109 | Stanford Ave | D3 109 |

# TO DO:

## Play the 'star' game

- Each player draws two 6 by 6 grids, and labels the rows 1 to 6, and the columns A to F.
- Each player, unseen by the other, draws 6 stars, each in a different square of one grid.
- Take turns to find where your opponent's stars are by guessing a square: for example, C2.
- Record your guesses on your other grid.
- The winner is the first player to guess the position of all 6 stars.

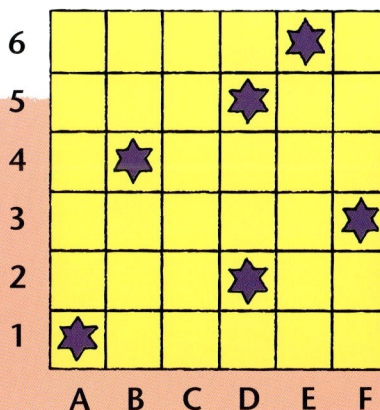

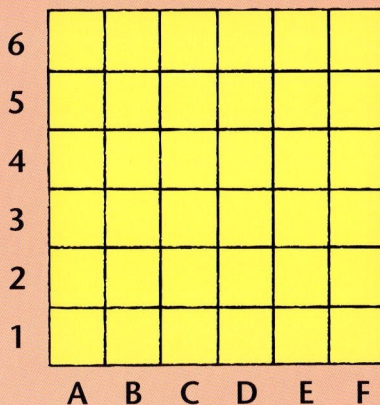

37

# 18 COORDINATES

A **coordinate grid** is another way of locating position. Instead of labelling the rows and columns, the lines of the grid are numbered.

The vertical lines are numbered from left to right. The horizontal lines are numbered from bottom to top. The numbered vertical line is called the **vertical axis**. The numbered horizontal line is called the **horizontal axis**. Together, they are called the **coordinate axes**.

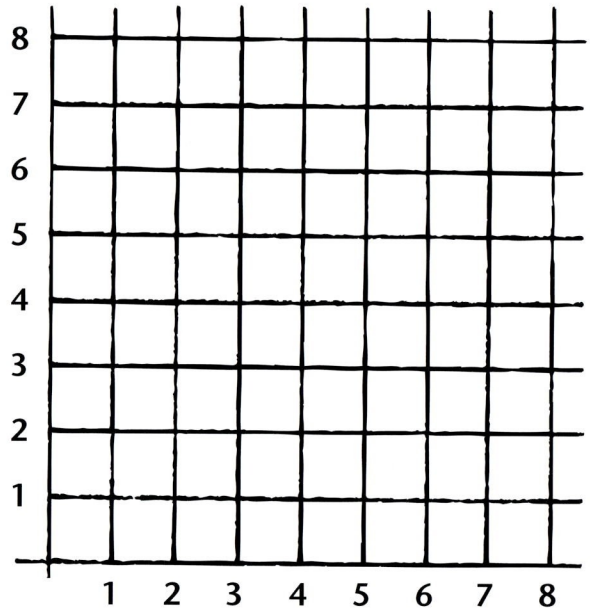

The point P has: a **horizontal coordinate** of 3, and a **vertical coordinate** of 4. In mathematical short-hand, we say that P has **coordinates** (3, 4).

The first number in the pair is always the horizontal coordinate, and the second is the vertical co-ordinate.

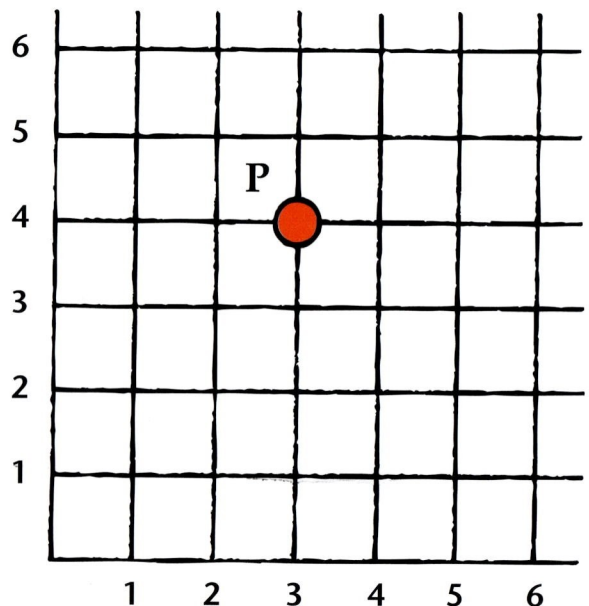

# CHALLENGE:

This rectangle is drawn by joining the points:
(2, 4), (5, 7), (7, 5), (4, 2).

Can you discover what shapes are made by joining these points?
First shape:
(2, 1), (6, 1), (6, 5), (2, 5)
Second shape:
(3, 2), (6, 2), (3, 5)
Third shape:
(1, 4), (2, 2), (4, 2), (5, 4)

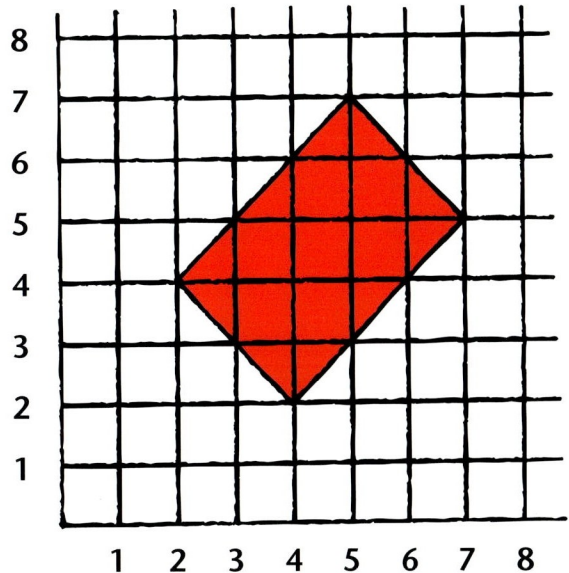

# TO DO:

## Play the 'three in a line' game

You need a partner, and a coordinate grid, like this, drawn on squared paper. You also need a red dice and a blue dice. Each player uses a different-coloured pencil.

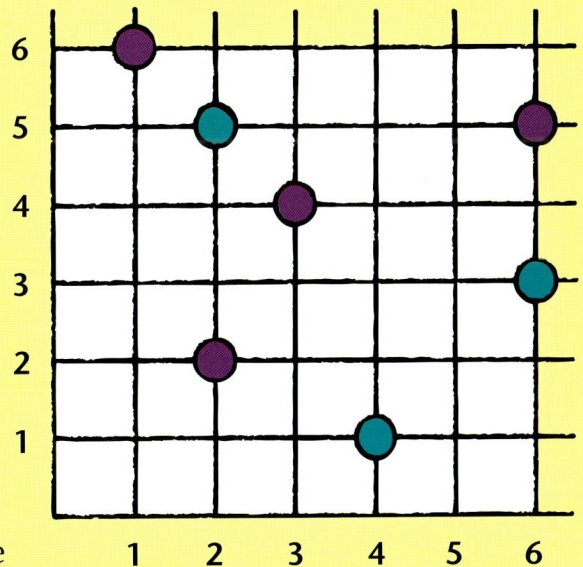

- The number on the red dice shows the horizontal coordinate.
- The number on the blue dice shows the vertical coordinate.
- Take turns to throw both dice, then plot the resulting point, in your colour, on the grid.
- The winner is the first player to have three of their points lying on a straight line horizontally, vertically or diagonally.

39

# 19 DIRECTION

A **magnetic compass** is an instrument for measuring direction. It contains a magnetic needle which always points in the direction North.

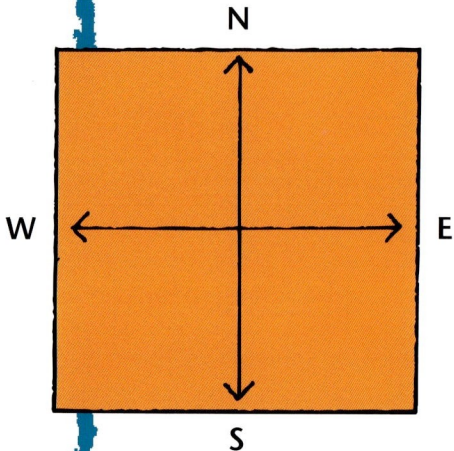

N

W ← → E

S

The main direction points are North, South, East and West. It is common to write N, S, E and W in shorthand. North and South are in opposite directions. East and West are also in opposite directions.

Most maps are drawn so that the direction North is vertically upwards on the page.

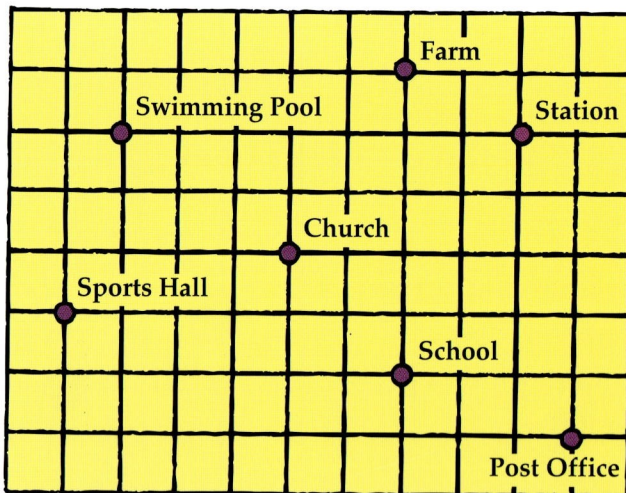

Farm

Swimming Pool

Station

Church

Sports Hall

School

Post Office

The scale of this map is 1 cm to 1 mile.

*Start at the church, move 4 miles East, 2 miles South, 7 miles West, then 4 miles North. Where have you arrived?*

## TO DO:

Invent your own route from the sports hall to the station.

There are direction points half way
between each of the main direction points.
The direction half way between North and
East is North-East (NE).
The other points are North-West (NW),
South-East (SE) and South-West (SW).

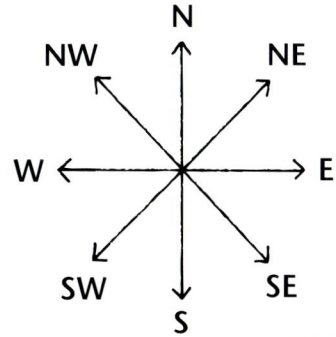

## TO DO:

### Make a paper compass

- Take a large square piece of paper.
- Fold it into quarters, then fold it again diagonally.
- Open it out, and use a ruler to draw the 8 compass directions along the fold lines.
- Use a magnetic compass to find the direction North.
- Place your paper compass on the floor or table, so that your North is pointing in the right direction.
- Now write down two things in the room which lie in the North direction and two which lie in each of the South, East and West directions.

## TO DO:

### Play the direction game

This is a game for two players.
You need some squared paper each.

- One player draws a hidden shape using vertical, horizontal and diagonal lines.
- They then describe it to the other player, using directions: for example, start at A and draw along 3 squares East, then 2 diagonals South-East, then 2 squares South, then 5 squares West, and 4 squares North, to finish.
- The other player draws the shape from these directions.
- Now compare the two shapes to see if they are identical.
- Play again, but swap roles.

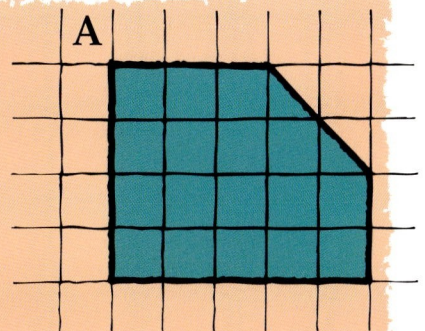

# 20 BEARINGS

A **bearing** is a way of showing direction.
It is always measured from North in a clockwise direction.
Bearings are written with three figures and measured in degrees. Here are some examples:

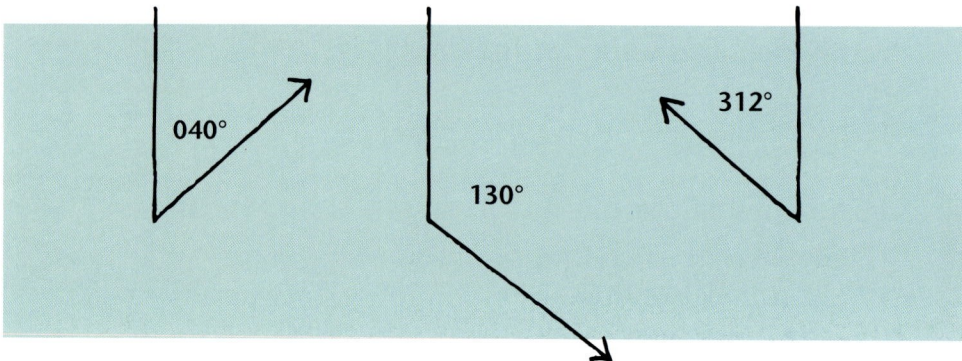

So: the direction East is the same as a bearing of 090°
the direction South is the same as a bearing of 180°
the direction West is the same as a bearing of 270°.

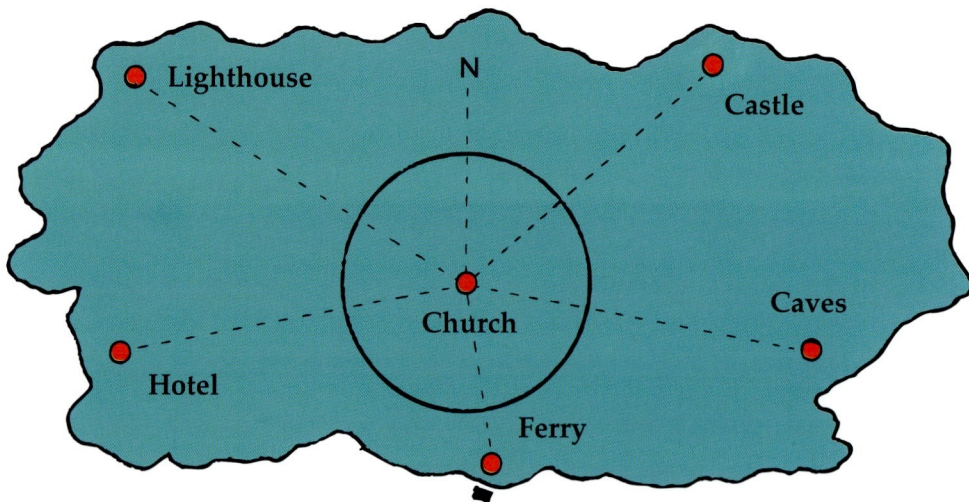

If you are standing at the church, then the direction of other points on the island can be described by their bearings. The bearing of the castle from the church is 040°. The caves are on a bearing of 100°, and the ferry 170°.

## CHALLENGE:

Can you say the bearings of the hotel and the lighthouse from the church?

The picture shows a ship's radar aerial. The radar sends out a signal which bounces off objects it meets, like another ship or an island. These signals rebound and are picked up by the aerial. Inside the ship there is a radar screen, which is like a television screen. The signals picked up by the radar are shown as white blips on the screen.

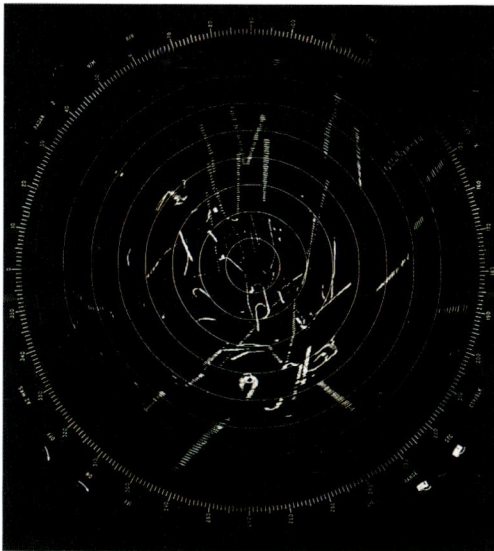

The picture on the screen has bearings marked from 000° to 360° round a set of circles. The position of a blip on the screen shows the bearing and distance of the object from the ship.

## CHALLENGE:

The bearing of SE is 135°. Can you say the bearings of South-West, North-East and North-West?

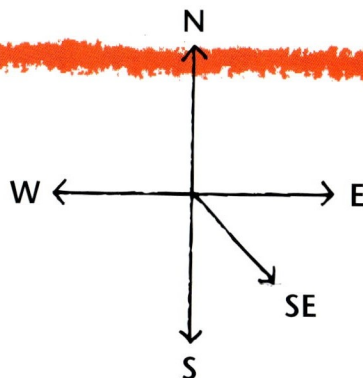

# GLOSSARY

| | |
|---|---|
| **acute angle** | An angle which measures less than a right angle. |
| **angle** | An amount of turn. |
| **anti-clockwise** | The opposite direction to clockwise. |
| **area** | The amount of surface space used by a two-dimensional object. |
| **bearing** | It describes the direction of something. |
| **capacity** | A measure of how much a container holds. |
| **clockwise** | Turning in the direction in which clock hands move. |
| **coordinate grid** | A grid to locate position. |
| **coordinates** | A pair of numbers which locate a position of a point on a coordinate grid. |
| **cubic centimetre** | A cube whose edges are one centimetre. |
| **cubic metre** | A cube whose edge is one metre. |
| **degrees** | Units for measuring angles. |
| **diagonal line** | A line which joins two vertices of a shape. |
| **enlargement** | An enlargement of a shape is a larger copy. |
| **grid** | A rectangle arrangement of squares. |
| **hexagon** | A polygon with six sides. |
| **horizontal lines** | Straight lines drawn from left to right on the paper. |
| **kite** | A quadrilateral with two pairs of adjacent equal sides. |
| **litre** | A measure of capacity. One thousand cubic centimetres. |
| **magnetic compass** | An instrument for measuring direction. |
| **obtuse angle** | An angle which measures more than one right angle and less than two right angles. |

| | |
|---|---|
| **parallel lines** | Lines which, if extended, will never cross. |
| **parallelogram** | A quadrilateral with two pairs of parallel sides. |
| **pentagon** | A polygon with five sides. |
| **perimeter** | The distance around the boundary of a shape. |
| **plan** | A drawing of a view seen from above. |
| **polygon** | A two-dimensional shape with straight sides. |
| **protractor** | An instrument for measuring angle. |
| **quadrilateral** | A polygon with four sides. |
| **reflex angle** | An angle which measures more than two right angles. |
| **right angle** | A quarter turn. |
| **scale drawing** | A plan or map drawn in smaller proportion to the real size. |
| **set-square** | An instrument used to draw, and check for, right angles. |
| **tessellate** | Shapes tessellate if they fit together snugly without leaving any spaces between them. |
| **vertical lines** | Straight lines drawn from the top to bottom, at right angles to a horizontal line. |
| **vertices** | The point at which two straight lines meet: the corners. |
| **volume** | The amount of space used by a three-dimensional object. |

# INDEX

# ANSWERS

**p5**  The roundabout is turning clockwise.
15 minutes, 30 minutes

**p7**  **Challenge**:

**Challenge**:
9 o'clock, 3 o'clock and 6 o'clock

**p8**  Acute angles

**p9**  **Challenge**:
(from left to right)
Shape 1: 4 right angles
Shape 2: 4 right angles
Shape 3: 3 acute angles and 1 reflex angle
Shape 4: 2 acute angles and 2 obtuse angles
Shape 5: 2 acute angles and 2 obtuse angles
Shape 6: 3 acute angles and 1 reflex angle
Shape 7: 1 right angle, 1 acute angle and 2 obtuse angles
Shape 8: 1 right angle, 2 acute angles and 1 obtuse angle

**Challenge**:
Right angle: 3 o'clock, 9 o'clock
Acute angle: 1 o'clock, 2 o'clock, 10 o'clock, 11 o'clock
Obtuse angle: 4 o'clock, 5 o'clock, 7 o'clock, 8 o'clock

The blue rectangle uses most space.

**p11**  **To do**:
The angle is 60°

**p12**  **To do**:
The 3 angles total 180°

**p13**  **To do**:
The 4 angles total 360°

**p16**  18 cm$^2$ and 20 cm$^2$

**p17**  **Challenge**:

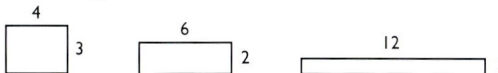

**p19**  **Challenge**:

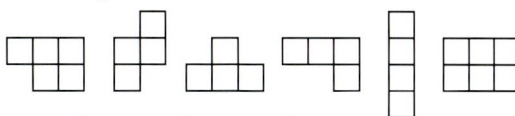

**p21**  30 cm$^3$, 27 cm$^3$, 16 cm$^3$
**Challenge**: 24 cm$^3$, 30 cm$^3$, 24 cm$^3$

**p27**

**Challenge**:
Shapes 1, 3 and 4 have 2 pairs of parallel lines
Shape 2 has 1 pair of parallel lines
Shapes 1 and 4 have perpendicular lines

**p28**

The pattern is a set of multiples of 11.

**p29**

A regular pentagon has 5 diagonals, a regular hexagon has 10.

**To do**:
The triangles are all the same isosceles triangles

**p31**

**Challenge**:
1, 8, 27, 64 cubes

**p33**

**To do**:
The distance between a) Mouse Hole and Danes Mill is about 2.25 kilometres b) Mount Pleasant and Norman's Green is about 2.5 kilometres.

**p34**

Clockwise: teapot, washing-up liquid, bowl, drink can, cup, (centre) saltcellar

**p36**

**Challenge**:
Caves – G4; lighthouse – A6; hotel – C3

**p39**

**Challenge**:
Square, triangle, trapezium

**p40**

Swimming pool

**p42**

The hotel has bearings of 280°; lighthouse has bearings of 305°

**p43**

Challenge: 225°, 045°, 315°